A Fire in the Sunset

A Decade of Love Poems

Moses Yuriyvich Mikheyev

First published by Moses Yuriyvich Mikheyev in February 2024
Copyright © Moses Yuriyvich Mikheyev 2024
All rights reserved.

979-8-9880100-4-3 (Paperback)
979-8-9880100-3-6 (eBook)

Cover design by Iliyana of Wonderburg Creations
Edited by Janie Mills
Formatted by Polgarus Studio

to all the women
past and present
who have made
poets like me possible

Our love has wrinkles
as old as the Earth.

Loving you *was* a miracle

       holding you, a miracle

Everything else

wasn't.

What are you?
memory, fragment, feat?
Did you pursue me from the past
or I you, from out of eternity?

How I wish
to feel your history
brush up against
the skin of my future

Our love is a Time Machine,
neither here nor there—
a breaking in the heart
yet to happen

I recollect you
in pieces, puzzles, poems
Enshroud you in verbs, nouns, adjectives
Associate you with expressions
like epic
        triumphant
            romantic
                beautiful
                    lovely

Desire I've dreamt ten thousand times
But not enough

For nothing is enough when I compare it to you
No love, no poem, no Time Machine

No century can hold you

But this mouth,
these hands . . .
Can they be your century made flesh?

Here! Beside me!
Come! Sit a while!
Stay!

Let a second from my clock keep you
We can lay beneath tarmac black
See stars sparkle
collect in clusters of color
Gathering words—grains of stardust—from
ages beyond
bestowing shine upon you

For no one can love you

      Not in this way
          Not in this age
              (Not in the one to come)

No one can love you but I

Ever since you left
the ocean has lost its shimmer
   And the sky was rolled up and carted away

The dog at the doorway barks incessantly
      And the neighbors no longer wave their friendly
hands
The sidewalk feels like quicksand,

                                feet taking

steps but still sinking

My mouth is stuck in a record we used to play
                            when we were

young and fearless

Those wild summer days—

                        tongue wants to speak

but only lyrics

And then your arms rest on me,
    sinking entire seasons into my skin—
Where
    your onyx hair sighs and falls into
a deep slumber on slender shoulders
your jasmine skin curls up against the warmth of my
lips
        and my mouth draws out
patches of blue-love on your soft neck

Your rounded cheeks are goblets of rosy wine,
        and your skin is
            perfumed with the magic
of a hundred vineyards

Your eyebrows are black
        like twilight
                    and curved
            like the sunset darkness swallows
Your brown eyes are
                    as still as night—
                    yet in their Spanish waters, I
see Armadas sinking
Your ears are mine,
        saving secrets brought
            on winds that whisper
        Your lips are

petals plucked
    from
        flowers in ripened sky—

                ruby-red,

they smell of cherries

Your breasts are
        heaps of fruit
        in baskets
    and the nectar of your navel is

             a waterhole

of wonder

"Oh, will you tempt me forever?" you mutter
And I whisper back, "Where'd you come from?"

For there is this—

Breath after rapturous breath,
       you arch your back
         while I
        fling open the sky
            and let the stars

                  drop
                  down

                                        on us
Between your legs
                        I press my tongue
                                    and watch your
leaves change color

As one age follows another,
                                so do I follow you
from place to place—
                        until I, too, collapse

 inside your

            labyrinth of love

Slowly the cosmos settles into the couch of your royal
body,

                    and you grasp for bedsheets
            and linens
                        and pillows

Yet your strong back cradles
            the weight of my slain
                    body—and you, O Sorceress,
breathe myth into my soul

And we start again

                where the end has no beginning

where autumn blooms
       and spring turns gold

And I gaze at you like I've lost a part of Eden
Idle summer days wasted on sands near your ocean
Once upon a time
Time lay curled up,
twisted into itself
Sleeping soundlessly
We didn't want to wake it

For who knew what would happen then?

But we sank our teeth into forbidden fruit—
and Time came to us, out of the storm,
baring fangs and funerals

Now, as an adult, as a man chased by Time
I suppose everything that's oh-so-bad happens there

Summer slips into decades that die on dead-end streets
Grape skin turns raisin (without wine)
Once-smooth lips become leathered with long age
There's no escaping it—not even for a second
It counts your days out like a mathematician
The numbers don't always carry over
And when they do
Mistakes occur—never in your favor
We pray for another whimsical weekend we could
waste

like ten-year-olds
But Time never sleeps—not like it used to,
not like when we were children

It's a cruel thing. Time is.
It takes what it cannot give back
Occasionally, morsels drop off its tables like manna
Lucky we are to ask and luckier still to receive
"Beggars can't be choosers," they said
You only get Time when you don't want it
And when you do
My God, it'll hurt

As for us
there's only an impending sense of doom partially
mitigated by temporal flakes of love

we are mere numbers being crunched and crushed by
a calculator,
by a mathematician feigning magician
who forgot how to disappear

If only we could put Time to sleep
So that I could spend
Uncounted moments and timeless seasons of unmeasured
magic
with you

Having lost nothing
not Eden, not love
not your scent lingering on lips, leaves, branches, trees
in that dreamy garden,
that pre-temporal paradise

Time needs a lullaby
But I sing to it from outside the city walls
in a tongue She does not comprehend

of Time
we do not speak
what we don't know
and never will

Spellbinding stars sink
   into the earth below
bringing with them
      the moon, the universe—and Aphrodite

—light drips from the moon-crescent
      and splashes into
      the blue milk of the Pacific

This August night you

            follow
            me

barefoot into the ocean
      we swim in galaxies of supernovas and space-
time

Only the gods know what we'll find there

The mirror-eyes of the ocean observe your moonlit
skin
   I hold my breath.
         no longer do I wonder why
            the clay of your body attracts
            stardust,

hands,
weekends

—for entire galaxies swirl into being like love out of
thin air
and then settle on your lips like manna
and I open my mouth
to eat of your fruit

Only dreams know what I'll taste there

I'll remember you, Paris
if only in poems
that'll haunt me like the
rhythmic rhyming of your rain
drops falling onto the hardwood floors
beside my bedroom window
Outside stands Eiffel, guarding whatever remains of
my heart
How much have I left here?
How much have I reclaimed?

Hours ago—before my plane scraped its tires against
your earth,
before sparks flew
—I had known you,
Paris
only in pictures, in pixels, in approximations

But now—
O, full-bodied wine of a woman whom I shall drink
I'll pour you like champagne into this crystal cup
Swallow you like a mouth in love
Have your way with me
Intoxicate, intoxicate!
Seduce me like the others
Why, I'm a virgin—but only for you!

You, O, You who are composed of starlight
and seasons that stretch greedy hands into
months of Parisian past,
centuries of churches and cathedrals and catechisms
you rest on

You have a millennia of experience
and ten million dreams that light up your towers

But in my bedroom
beside this small window
beside *You*

I'm kept company by few

                                        postcards, poems,
placeholders

                            brightened by a lonely bulb

And I—
Well, I only have you

It's only been three days—and some say
one should not miss another during so brief a period

Maybe they're right.

But I miss the scent of jasmine on my palms

—for I'd rather cradle your face in my hands

        between a thousand constellations
            between red rose and iron thorn

than miss you so.

From first whispers to last caress
    hands helplessly amusing themselves
with the truth of you

Arms strong, shoulders stronger
    your chin resting on me
Lips perched near my neck

Mind wandering—will I kiss you or not?
"It's a pleasant evening," murmured softly
    Stars turn to listen
And sit down,
        crossed-legged constellations
catch their own breath
and bury
        it quietly in a delicate breeze
a stream of words on
    a seldom-made
        trip to the tongue
Thoughts held captive in your dazzling presence
    "May I, my lady?"

Eyes closed, shutting
        Gates of Heaven
eyelashes cease their inexplicable explorations

With arms strong and shoulders stronger

I wrap myself in
    summer
       scents
         of a blossomed you

Moonlight washing up against our fragile bodies
   Stars collapsing from eager expectation

  as I touch
        taste
            tremble
between passionate
  mouthfuls of your truth

A thousand misplaced kisses

     —and yet—

  only one of you

When it is quiet
  and all I hear

                is the sound of dreams flowing
                  into and out of color

Then—

you walk in
  barely shouldering a thin-strapped dress

      your long legs step over
                        years and years

of black and white

A breezy night,
   a stir in a moment
      small talk made
amidst a bustling crowd of boisterous noise

"Is that the place over there?"

Arm in arm
   you whirl me 'round
a city made of dancing towns

and waltz me down a corridor
into your charming universe

And in that instant
—five minutes of you—
I am in love forever

—and then time became precious

we held onto it, cradling it in our arms like baby-skin

as if

it would crease
   the moment we'd
      unclench our fists

countless summers disappeared into the fold of our soul

The lake waters and I lap at the feet of your love
    and fill your mouth with welcome dew

—for you've had
this thirst that burned
from Julys spent on

salt
and tears
and black concrete

that splattered hot,
tar on romance

and your skin, peeled from a sun that filled my cup
then yours
then spilled over

into hands that tried to grasp
the escaping-loves that once sighed

...*before* jumping off cliffs

into the rocks below

Once upon a time I held your fragile body
raindrops rolled over your tired skin
and a wet dog tried to cause the
once-bitten-twice-shy
But I had already bitten into you,
my fruit of passion
beneath stormy August and July sky

Where were we, then, on that night?
Did you hold me to pieces,
or did I somehow escape you, like Houdini
slipping through your garden, stealing
memories of us in Eden
making love to the sound of God
searching, breathing, seeking
the two of us out?

They said, "All pretty things must end"
with voices dipped in contrition (while you and I
were still together)

But we—
gazed into each other's eyes, believing
that over the sunset lay another sea
full of misplaced kisses with youth unceasing
just pleading to be dreamed

Drown me.
Drown me.
Drown me.

Drown me in the fountains

   of your love

     and may my breath be found

beneath your oceans

Kiss me!
Kiss me with the wrinkles of your lips
brush away
acres and acres

   of pain
      and hurt
         and the unrequited

stretched as far as the eye can see

Comfort me, comfort me

with the comfort of your warmth

—for I too, have loved

—and then
our lips met for the first time, and
our mouths widened
        with sweet expectation.

Our eyes closed
—for the sacred couldn't be seen, it could only be
experienced

in that still, small moment,
we both knew what it was
to be young and in love

Your beauty once wandered my streets, seeking—
all I had hoped for was
    a wrinkled moment,
        a gaze that lingered

  one that fell between
the Abyss and the Sea

that separated us—

Could I be your Jacob?
I'd wrestle your pride to earth,
    plant it into this black dirt
that surrounds us both

You could sprout and bloom,
    like three flowers in June
        a trinity of inescapable wonder
            a garden woven into the fiber of Babylon
just begging to be hung
    people traveling to-and-fro
        watching,
            wondering:
"Will we ever know her secret?"

And I—I'd still be wrestling your grace

into this dirt that

made us both

'Tis spring again—
an Old Testament sheds its wineskins
in favor of the New

and all I can do is breathe
that scent of bloomed freshness
budding like magnolias
on brown branches bending toward earth

I stand watching
you from that ephemeral distance—

A space called Winter
where my own dirt is still frozen, unturned soil
—restless, aching soil—
reaching out for your warmth

Drag me!
Drag me across your fields
Stretch me!
Stretch me out beneath your blue sky
—and shine on me with the light of your pale-sun

Settle like April pollen
    onto my outstretched hands,
        palms face upward,
            eyes closed shut,
as I await the arrival of you

You.

You, my love, have turned
   the world to glass
—and now I see!

   Now I see what I had not seen before:

                          dreams being stolen from
out of the vault of the night sky

Sink
    mountains of touch
into my flesh

—for I am
but breaking of bread
    in your messianic hands

But I—

I hope to taste her
    to spill a wet kiss
those eyes a culture,
        a religious abyss

Invite me in—
    to a place where
mouth meets lips
        saying hello

And you recline,
    repose
    on a bed made of dreams that I once dreamt
        lie
        on thoughts that I once thought

It's all so easy for a girl like you,
living in a room
made by the words of a god who

used to speak

—but his lips
        his tongue
            his mouth

are *busy*

        now

I drew her up like water from a spring found flowing
With rains placed on amenable laps of summer
Where flowers bloomed explosions of radiant unknowing
And eyes that haunted mellow stars above her

Her eyes a deepest black of bluest seas
Hands trading in burnt bronze for pearls
Damn necklace torn from collar in ecstasy
Restless lips of mine find home eternal

I had her pressed against the ground like an iron plow
Her straps dropped like kernels into fertile black soil
Green valleys of rolling love on her naked brow
Kisses etching marks on her skin unspoiled

Near the desert regions of her sunshine navel
I found myself lurking in quenched exploration
That thirst of old and fragrant new, entangled
Her body, my body, in Edenic damnation

Did I ever know her, and she know me?
Or were we seasons on opposite ends of the year?
Always holding hands at a distance of two trees
One blooming summer and the other budding spring

Strange how
something so brittle, so insignificant
—a soft kiss, a tender whimper—
could become an age unto itself

a thousand years of smoke blossoms into
a fire in the sunset

and she appears,
out of the whirlwind
her dress, coals of red

If only love were a place one could stay—

                              I'd take you there

we could drive down dirt roads
        where dust swirls
and turns kisses into mud

Sure, we'd be tainted,
                        children of clay

but together

my lips would be yours
my mouth would be yours
and somewhere in the midst of this Middle-Earth

You would keep me

                        and quietly murmur, "Stay"

—If only love were a place one could

Stay.

When my shoulders sunk low
and my eyes were folded
When I no longer believed that
my hands could bring comfort to another Her

It was you who envisioned a smile where there was a
stone
   and from between my lips
you called out the sacred

So, if I should ever love again
   I will remember—and love you as you had
      once loved me

Sometimes when I dream—
I think of:
a garden in the sky
full of stars
I dig up sparks with bare hands
expose their shine and their shiver
just to impress you
while you wait for 11:11
to make a wish
about longer summer nights, teeming with laughter
tears held back
but warm water, nonetheless
joy in all of its manifestations
colors trapped in drops of light
dripping from the corners of your bright eyes
holding hands, sipping milkshakes, wondering
if we'd stay
      together,
like smoke and fire,
like stars and twinkle

somewhere in the deep-black,
the haze of time
where even moonlight sits down to rest,
lays its head on your curved neck
"Light sleeps darkly, does it not?"

I pull apart a kiss
from your folding fruit
   wonder of wonders
      holy of holies

let me make love to you
let me explore this tender earth
let me uncover
   this shine and shiver
that is buried in the bends of your bare skin

Our first kiss managed to make magic
and out of the trick—a romance
a girl so impossibly beautiful
all the winds and seasons and seas had to stop—and
look over their shoulder
while I held you with infinite tenderness
loving on you
God, I could spend eternity waiting for you to love
me back

I could get you into my Scriptures
Slide your words between the Old and the New
Priests frightened by perishable heresies
Pews warmed over by bodies no longer listening
But feeling—Oh, God—feeling, feeling
Yes, feeling that blood-heat of red love
I'm hoping there's a church altar I could take you to
—one where you whisper, "I Do"
one where we say, "Forever and Ever and Ever"
where your mistakes turn into wine I drink

But I sit still. These days, I sit still.

I loved you, love you, and will love you.

Could you find me?
I'll change numbers and postal codes just to sleep

near you
I'll slay passions and lay cold knives to rest
Just let me kiss your brutal, brutal lips

Betray me, you Judas.
Call the cops! you cruel, cruel woman
And I swear I'll love you till they arrive
till they place handcuffs on these hands
that once roamed the barren warmth of your body
that once made you sing Hallelujah

I have all of these memories—but no mind to hold
them
All of these poems—yet no lips that know them

And I—
I only wish to give you something I've never had
"Here," I whisper, "Take it.
For this—this could hold the both of us."

You get on a plane and fly great distances
my soul stretches after you,
                    a banner of love

And you wonder if I still think of you
your laugh, your smile, your small hands sitting still
near the bend of your hips

Tonight, I'll be crying softly,
hoping nobody hears
I don't want you to know how soft I am
how unlike the others I am
how I bruise easily where others inflict pain

In another life,
in a time weaved from the whispers of bedroom love
we'd be made from the earth of a single country,
and the gods would grant our feet a closer home

But here on this clay we walk,
cursed to live distant lives,
to watch the burning of separate lights

While your body is bathed in moonlight,
I toil beneath the heat of midday sun

To whom do I turn
to move these continents?

And who could drag Los Angeles to Russia?

He smells like cedars
   his broad shoulders made of pine trees

In the fold of his night
      there are dark forests, unseen
Smoke from his chimney rises
and fog begs near his calloused feet

Sometimes he mutters something
incredibly soft
—silk clouds made of dandelions—
and his words patch
her stubborn heart

Deep in that wooded forest
   there sits an open meadow

   And in-between the night and dark
      there is a pond that's filled with dreams
I'd once seen a nude girl swim in its glowing waters

      that swirled
        and burst into light-beam

His eyes sparkle now.

There is nothing dull
                    or dry
                            or grey about him.

And the girl—she still swims.

Light trickles from the blue
puddle of stars
under our feet

Dethrone my arrogance
Your lips kiss with consciousness
Pull down my temples
        raze my heights
till they stoop low,
                    bowed before your own humility

For what am I without you, darling?

                —just a crack in your sidewalk

In the fast moment between
his eyes opening, seeing
flooded-mind image
                    made of ink drawn from her bone

every poem he had written
had become about
Her.

I stood before you
love in arms

and yet
exposed,
    vulnerable
        and so disarmed

Knocked softly on your front porch
    where the wisps of lemon meringue sugared the air

And the earth
    the ground upon which I stood, moved
and yet
the universe sat still.
    Silent.
        Waiting.

Birdsong stretched across purple sky

stretched—

until it could stretch—

no more

And when you opened your door

I had my name etched,
   etched
all over your bedposts,

a love left gasping on a bed full of holes

Your love is thievery—

stealing dreams from out of the night sky

I have fallen in love many times, many times

and always with you

The man who loved you
No longer lives
I came to his door this evening,
knocked
I saw cobwebs clothing heartaches
mail from you—scattered & unopened
Under the mat, a key—
its edges blunt
it no longer opens doors

I imagine one time
some summer night
You snuck out late
a few stars past midnight
Hung your tender heart
Waited
Restlessly placed the key and turned

And a man
Very much like myself
Only younger
Loved on you

I sometimes dream of him
But the dreams have locks
My keys are now blunt too

Hands clasp the yet-to-be,

wishing it were the here-and-now

fingers unbuttoning love

The stars grow tired,
shrug their shoulders,
and fall out of the sky,
wearing nothing but robes of comet-white

Is she not one of the stars?

She casts off her robes—steps into my room—and
composes constellations.

And time danced to a slowly dripping faucet
in a hotel bathroom
where the white sheets had their melancholic innocence

saturated with scents of you

All I could do
was hover near your vibrant presence
and pretend I did deserve
the skin cells
falling off that gorgeous face
into the threads and fibers below

This old, tired love
still grows bruises
still hopes for magic,
for youth to come and make
the valleys near those twinkling eyes disappear

But who am I to ask for resurrection?
I who am but a small soul
praying for a miracle

Sometimes I touch my skin

and wonder

if the past is all there ever was

Bulletproof mistress of made-up dreams

I'm all yours now
just seventeen

                    Finding my way to heaven through
the cracks in your skin

I'm yours.
                But only for a moment.

—for I give all that I am in an instant,
a vast expanse of eternity
between the small silence of words whispered

"Could you be my forever?"

How could I?

I who am eternal,
whose life is ever the Already-Not-Yet

. . . always giving myself to Another,
sinking years into seconds unspent

Love, a fragmentary thing—

begins mid-sentence

and ends with
the unmovable silence of a

period.

Author's Note

My written work is my body. My poems are my body. And like all bodies, my work has its scars, its blemishes, its fatal imperfections. I've learned to live with my work as much as I've learned to live with my body.

This is it.

Whatever happens, happens—and it happens to this body. Whatever bruises come, whatever joys, this body experiences them.

I've done my best to weed out the worst and polish the best. As for how well I've done—that is for future readers to decide.

I don't know.

And I don't think that knowing matters. It's also possible that I don't even care. Who said I chose this body? Who said I chose this work? I never claimed such an impossible thing.

All I've claimed is: *This is it.*

This is my work. These are my poems. This is my body. As for the rest? Does it even matter?

Of note, some of these poems have appeared in my novels (and some of them I've changed for this edition). Some may even appear in novels that have not yet been written. Who knows?

www.ingramcontent.com/pod-product-compliance
Lightning Source LLC
Chambersburg PA
CBHW060709030426
42337CB00017B/2823